Push and Pull

written by Maria Gordon
and
illustrated by Mike Gordon

Thomson Learning

New York

Simple Science

Day and Night
Float and Sink
Fun with Color
Fun with Heat
Fun with Light
Push and Pull

First published in the
United States in 1995 by
Thomson Learning
New York, NY

Published simultaneously in Great Britain
by Wayland (Publishers) Limited

Library of Congress Cataloging-in-Publication Data

Gordon, Maria.
  Push and pull / written by Maria Gordon and ;
illustrated by Mike Gordon.
        p.   cm. — (Simple science)
  Includes index.
  ISBN 1-56847-458-X. — ISBN 1-56847-462-8 (pbk.)
  1. Mechanics—Juvenile literature. [1. Mechanics—Experiments.
2. Experiments.] I. Gordon, Mike, ill. II. Title. III. Series: Simple
science (New York, N.Y.)
QC127.4.G67   1995
530.1'5—dc20 —dc20   95-11631

Printed in Italy

Contents

There are two ways to move things. You can push or pull them.

A push moves something away. Use your finger to move a toy car away from you. This is a push.

A pull moves something nearer. Grip the car with your finger and thumb. Move it toward you. This is a pull.

5

There are many different ways to push and pull.

Some pushing and pulling just happens...

like wind blowing...

plants growing...

and water flowing.

But people and animals can push or pull to do things, like gather food.

The things people make that push and pull are called machines. Some machines are very simple like…

…knives to push into things…

…belts to pull things tight…

…brooms to push things away.

Other machines are not as simple; for example...

...the ones pulling hands around a clock...

...motors pushing propellers around...

...or engines pushing rockets into space.

9

Long ago, cave people rubbed stones together to make fire. They hunted with spears. Later, people also shot stones and arrows. Rubbing, throwing, and shooting arrows are all kinds of pushing and pulling.

People invented many things to push and
pull, like paddles to push through water,
wheelbarrows to push heavy things, and
snow sleds pulled by dogs.

Many years ago a scientist named Isaac Newton watched an apple fall from a tree. He saw that there was something pulling the apple to the ground. He called it gravity.

You can see this for yourself. Hold out a ball and let go. Gravity pulls it to the ground.

If gravity didn't pull people and things down, they would float like astronauts in space!

Isaac Newton showed people important things about pushing and pulling. You can see them, too.

Put a toy car on a level, flat table. It stays still if it is not pushed or pulled.

A moving toy car keeps going in a straight line unless it is pushed or pulled by something.

A toy car moves when it is pushed or pulled.

Now try pushing or pulling one when it is moving. It will turn, slow down, or speed up.

Push a toy car over the edge of a table. Gravity pulls on it. This makes the car turn and fall.

When something is pushed or pulled, it pushes or pulls back! Heavy things push or pull back more than light ones. This is why they are harder to move.

Tie an empty plastic pail to a piece of string. Tie the other end of the string to a big, empty toy truck in the middle of a table. Put modeling clay in the pail until it begins to pull the truck.

Fill the truck with modeling clay. Now the truck is harder to pull. Put more clay in the pail to make it pull even more and move the truck.

Pushing and pulling can change the shape of things. Use your fingers to push and pull some modeling clay or dough and change its shape.

Make different shapes with your fingers.
Muscles in your arm are pulling
your finger bones.
Use your muscles to pull other bones.
What shapes can your body make?

When things are pushed or pulled, they rub against anything next to them. This is called friction.

Push a toy car on a smooth, flat floor. It cannot keep going for long because it rubs against the floor—and even the air.

AIR

20

Rough things make more friction. Push the toy car on a carpet. It does not go far.

In a real car, brakes rub against the wheels. This friction helps the car to stop. Smooth ice makes less friction and makes cars hard to stop.

Things that roll make less friction. They need smaller pushes and pulls to make them move.

Push a coin on its edge. Now push a coin lying flat. The first coin rolls. It needs less push.

Heavy things need bigger pushes and pulls to make them move. Push a ball. It rolls, but it needs more push than a coin on its edge.

Look at cars and trucks.
You can see that the big ones need
bigger engines to pull their wheels
around and make them move.

23

How much pushing and pulling do you do?

Your feet push against the ground when you run or walk.

Push the pedals on a bike.

With an adult, pull the oars on a boat. Watch the oars push against the water.

Pull the peel from an orange.

Push a toy car down a slope. Push against it to make it stop.

Pushing and pulling changes things around you.

Wind pushes trees and changes their shape. The sea pushes so long and hard it makes holes in rocks. Gravity changes the shape of the land when it pulls down rocks.

People and machines pull up plants from the land; bulldozers push earth around. Moving bikes, cars, and trucks can push into things and change their shape... and even yours!

What ways can you see pushing and pulling being used here?
The answers are on page 31.

1

2

3

4

5

Which things here need a big push or pull?
Where is friction being made?

Additional projects

Here are a few more projects to test out pushing and pulling. The projects go with the pages listed next to them. These projects are harder than the ones in the book, so be sure to ask an adult to help you.

4/5   Look for the push or pull behind the movements in simple, ordinary tasks such as turning the pages of this book.

6/7   Spot plants and tree roots pushing up through soil and sidewalks. Make a display showing how animals push and pull, such as an elephant's trunk, a bird's beak, and a cat's paw.

8/9   Look inside the workings of moving toys. Make levers with rulers. Use simple tools. Show how one movement is used to make another one.

10/11   Learn about different inventions from ancient times to the present and see how they use pushing or pulling.

14/15   Use toy cars to show connection between the strength of a push or pull and speed.

18/19   Ask a gym teacher to explain how the muscles push and pull. Do some exercise to see how your muscles work.

20/21   Sit and slide on polished floors and on carpeted ones. Go ice-skating. Ask an adult to explain why braking a car or bicycle on an icy road is dangerous.

22/23   Make a drawing of you playing your favorite sport. What parts of it involve pushing and pulling?

26/27   Learn about road safety.

28/29   Hold a tug-of-war!

Answers

These need pushing or pulling:

1. When you squeeze a nutcracker, it pulls shut on a nut and cracks it open.
2. A doorknob must be turned to open the door; turning is a push and a pull.
3. This machine pushes and pulls on a saw to cut through a pipe.
4. Ants can pull several times their own weight in food!
5. In a game of tug-of-war, each team tries to pull harder than the other.
6. This boy is being pulled up by a magnet. Find out more about magnets!
7. You use a pull to get crayons out of a box.
8. You sometimes see babies being pushed in strollers.
9. Elephants can push logs with their trunks.
10. Push-buttons work just that way—with a push!

Other books to read

Branley, Franklyn M. **Gravity Is a Mystery.** New York: HarperCollins Children's Books, 1986.

Sipiera, Paul. **I Can Be a Physicist.** I Can Be Books. Chicago: Childrens Press, 1991.

Ward, Alan. **Force and Energy.** Project Science. New York: Franklin Watts, 1992.

Index